I Can See a Sheep!

by Cameron Macintosh

OXFORD
UNIVERSITY PRESS

I can see a sheep.

2

The sheep is in the shed.

I can see a hen.

The hen rushes to the feed.

The hen is high up on a rail.

The duck pushes its feet.

The duck is in the reeds.
It might see a toad!

reed

I can see a goat.

The goat is in the pen.
It pushes the rail.

I can see a foal.

The foal passes me!

The foal is in the sun.

I can see a rabbit.

The rabbit is in the run.
It can see at night.

tail

I can see a dog.

14

The dog runs along the road.